Kids Who Walk on Volcanoes

Text and photos by Paul Otteson

John Muir Publications
Santa Fe, New Mexico

Dedicated to the children and families of the Central American highlands.

John Muir Publications, P.O. Box 613, Santa Fe, NM 87504
Text and cover © by 1996 John Muir Publications
Photos © 1996 by Paul Otteson
All rights reserved.

Printed in the United States of America
First edition. First printing October 1996

Editors: Rob Crisell, Peggy Schaefer
Design: Marie J.T. Vigil
Production: Marie J.T. Vigil, Nikki Rooker
Printing: Guynes Lithographers

Distributed to the book trade by
Publishers Group West
Emeryville, California

Map illustration: Oliver Williams
Cover butterfly photo: Ree Strange Sheck
Title page: A volcano peeks through the mist near Antigua, Guatemala

Library of Congress Cataloging-in-Publication Data
Otteson, Paul.
    Kids who walk on volcanoes / by Paul Otteson.
        p.   cm.
    Summary: Describes the activities of Central American children—their work, their play, and their celebrations.
        ISBN 1-56261-308-1
        1. Children—Central America—Social conditions—Juvenile literature.
    2. Central America—Juvenile literature. 3. Volcanoes—Central America—Juvenile literature.
    [1. Central America—Social life and customs.] I. Title.
    HZ792.C35087   1996
    305.23'09728—dc20   96-26513
                                                                CIP
                                                                AC

Oliver Williams

◄ Most volcanoes in Central America are located in the western sections of Guatemala, El Salvador, Honduras, Nicaragua, and Costa Rica. This book highlights the children and cultures of these areas.

Kids Who Walk on Volcanoes

In lots of ways, the kids who live near the volcanoes of Central America are just like you. They learn new things every day. They work hard to help their families. They play and explore with friends.

In other ways, they are different. Some volcano-country kids have to earn money at hard jobs like adults. Some wear clothes that might look strange to you. They eat foods you aren't used to eating. They speak languages you might not understand. But the biggest difference between most kids in the United States and kids from the highlands of Central America, is that when they go outside on a clear day, they can see . . .

As a parade in Guatemala winds through the city streets, a volcano pokes through the clouds. →

Volcanoes!

More than 350 volcanoes dot the highlands along the Pacific Coast of Central America, including at least 20 that are active. Active volcanoes smoke, steam, and rumble. Hot pools and bubbling mud often surround them. Once in awhile, these active volcanoes erupt!

When a volcano erupts, ash and smoke billow into the sky and the earth shakes. Hot

Beware of bubbling mud pots! When water flows onto magma and hot rock underground, it turns into steam. The steam then bubbles up through the mud.

winds blow gritty clouds over the land. Cinders rain down upon cities, towns, and farms. Sometimes, red-hot lava flows down the sides of the volcano.

Many kids in Guatemala, El Salvador, Nicaragua, and Costa Rica live near active volcanoes. Most of these kids will never have anything to fear from eruptions or earthquakes, but sometimes volcanic activity can mean danger. Can you imagine living next door to an active volcano? You would never know when it might blow its top!

Most kids in Central America live around volcanoes all their lives. Their homes, schools, and churches sit right next to volcanoes. When the ground shakes and a volcano roars and smokes, they just keep working and playing. After all, even active volcanoes are quiet most of the time. Big eruptions are rare.

Volcano Agua **silently overlooks a town in ➔ Guatemala. This volcano isn't active these days, but someday it might erupt again.**

Down on the Farm

Lots of kids in volcano country live in small villages surrounded by fields and farms. These country kids have to become expert farmers. Farmers in the highlands grow beans, corn, coffee, fruit, and vegetables in the rich volcanic soil. On many farms, there are no machines or tractors to help with the work.

Everyone has to pitch in to get the job done, including kids.

During harvest time, farm workers pick coffee beans by hand and then dry them in the sun. They gather corn and fruit and pack them into boxes. Vegetables must be harvested at just the right time so they are fresh for markets in nearby cities and villages. Some foods grown in Central America are sold and

shipped to other countries, including the United States. That means kids your age might have helped grow the fruits and vegetables you eat.

Lots of families in poorer parts of Central America work on big farms owned by wealthy landlords. In exchange for their work, landlords let farmers use part of the land to grow what they need to live. Families often live in small, crowded houses that landlords give them. They might have yards for chickens and small gardens. With the money they earn, they buy food, and other essentials at the market. The majority of farms in Central America are too small to support big families. While some family members do the farm work, others take jobs in town.

← **Herding sheep can be a tough job.**

A Mayan girl helps pick coffee beans. →

7

City Kids

Many big towns and cities are very close to active volcanoes, such as Xela in Guatemala, Santa Ana in El Salvador, León in Nicaragua, and San José in Costa Rica. In many city families, everyone has a job. It's important for each member of the family to help earn money to pay for the things they need. Sometimes a father will work in a factory while the mother runs a small store. An aunt might work in an office while an uncle builds a house. It's different for each family.

Kids work, too. In poorer families, children might not be able to go to school because their parents need them to help. Sometimes, one or two kids in a family complete school, but the rest can't because their family needs them to earn money. In Central America, kids understand why they must work, but many of them also wish they could go to school. Some of them even dream of living like American kids. Like you, they are glad when the work is done and they can rest or play. However, they know how important it is to help their families.

← When a mother sells fabric and clothing at the market, her baby comes along.

In Central America, people buy food and → household items at outdoor markets.

Having Fun

Kids everywhere like to play. Friends gather in the school yard or town plaza to have fun. They play with brothers and sisters in the yard or on a quiet street in their neighborhood. Maybe there's a playground where they can swing and climb. Do you know kids who roller skate and jump rope where you live? If you lived in the Central American highlands, you could do all of these things with friends.

It takes three strong kids to get this ball rolling.

Nicaraguan kids play in the warm ocean water.

Kids enjoy playing at the beach, and there are lots of beaches in Central America! Did you know that many beaches in this land come from volcanoes? Over thousands of years, as rain falls on volcanoes, the rushing water wears away the dark volcanic rock, washing black sand and grit into streams and rivers. Eventually, the rivers carry all that sand to the ocean. Waves wash the sand onto the beaches. It's no wonder there are so many black sand beaches in Central America.

Kids also play and swim in lakes, ponds, and streams. They climb on rocks and roll down hills. There are all sorts of places to hide. Maybe they pretend that they are monsters who live in volcanoes and eat rocks! All they need are good imaginations.

That balloon is out of reach— unless you have friends to help! ➤

Some kids don't need toys to have fun.

Sports and Recreation

Can you think of anything more fun than playing games and sports with friends? With enough players for two teams, kids in the Central American highlands can play a good game of *fútbol* (FEWT-bowl) or "soccer," as we call it in the United States. Fútbol is the most popular sport in Central America. Kids learn to play when they are very young. If there isn't a fútbol field nearby, they play in a yard, or maybe on a quiet street. All they need is a ball and some space. The best fútbol players join national teams that play in the Olympics and other international competitions.

Fútbol isn't the only game in town. Kids also play basketball, baseball, and other sports. In Guatemala, there might be a basketball hoop by the church. In Nicaragua, there is a baseball field in every town. Every year, a few of the best baseball players in Central America move to the United States to play in the Major Leagues.

◄ Don't lose your balance when you skate!

Kids enjoy playing games together in school. On the plaza, it's more fun to skate if you can do it with a friend. At the park, it takes two to seesaw. If you play alone, no one will catch the ball when you throw it.

Some kids in volcano country enjoy playing together at summer camp. At camp, they learn and explore with kids their own age. Teamwork is important in many camp activities. What do you do if something is too heavy to lift or too high to reach? Get some friends to help you! Most kids can't go to camp because they are too poor or they have to work. But they can still have fun. As long as there are brothers, sisters, and friends around, there will always be ways to play together.

Fútbol (soccer) is the most popular sport in → Central America.

13

Let's Go See

There's a lot to learn in volcano country. When kids here get curious, they like to go exploring.

Should we peek behind those rocks?
Does it make sense when a parrot talks?
Is there treasure in that old box?

Let's

    go

      see.

Iguanas like this one live in the forests of Central America.

← **Guess where these Scouts are hiking? On an active volcano!**

Do I see a sloth in that tree so high?
That beetle crawls, but can it fly?
If we climb a hill, can we touch the sky?

Let's

go

see.

What washed up on the warm black sand?
How many toes on a lizard's hand?
Are flowers red in lava land?

Let's

go

see.

**Volcano country is filled with lots of brightly →
colored plants.**

Did an ancient Mayan make this mark?
Are those teeth from an old dead shark?
What could live in that cave so dark?

Follow me!

15

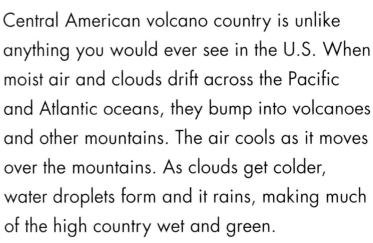

Nature in Lava Land

Central American volcano country is unlike anything you would ever see in the U.S. When moist air and clouds drift across the Pacific and Atlantic oceans, they bump into volcanoes and other mountains. The air cools as it moves over the mountains. As clouds get colder, water droplets form and it rains, making much of the high country wet and green.

Cloud forests grow high atop the mountains. For many days at a time, they are covered in mist and rain. Even when it's not raining, clouds and fog wrap the forests like blankets. On the mountainsides, tall trees spread their leaves and block out the sun. Down below, herbs, ferns, and mosses grow in the dim light. Howler monkeys climb through the branches looking for fruit and leaves to

The thick mountain rain forests of Central America are home to hundreds of different plants and animals.

Many rare butterflies flutter through the rain forests of Central America.

eat. Red macaws and green parrots chatter among the branches as insects look for food.

In the dry country west of the mountains, you might see an iguana sunning itself on a log. Maybe you'll meet an agouti, a peccary, or a coatimundi. These furry animals all live in the forests of Central America. Deep in the rain forest, jaguars raise their young and hunt for dinner. Remember to watch out for snakes!

Closer to the Pacific Ocean, snowy-white egrets perch on trees in mangrove swamps. Small crabs scurry across the sand. Sometimes sea turtles swim onto the beach at night to lay eggs. Early the next morning, they return to their homes in the ocean.

When wild lands are destroyed to make room for farms, many animals are left with no homes and nowhere to go to. A hundred years ago, there were countless wild plants and animals all over Central America. Now that much of the wild land is gone, so are dozens of species of birds, insects, and mammals.

Wild turkeys don't fly well, but they are very colorful.

Living with History

Just like kids in the United States, children in Central America learn about history. They study history in school. They listen to their parents and grandparents. When they grow up and have to make important decisions, they will need to know what happened long before they were born.

The first people of Central America arrived about 20,000 years ago. These early tribes lived in the rain forests, hunting animals and gathering fruit and other plants to eat. They were nomadic, which means they moved from place to

← **The Mayans built their pyramids hundreds of years before Spanish soldiers arrived. This pyramid is in Guatemala.**

place in search of food. When these Native Americans learned how to farm and grow crops, they stopped moving and settled down. Soon, villages traded with one another for things they needed, such as food, metal, and precious stones. A few tribes became large and powerful, growing into great civilizations.

The Mayan civilization was the first to build big cities and temples in the northern half of Central America. They were also the first people anywhere in North or South America to use a written language. You can learn about how they lived by examining the symbols and signs they carved into walls and pillars. If you visit Guatemala, you can explore Mayan ruins and see the courts where they played a game that was like a mix of basketball and soccer. You might learn how they built palaces and temples for their kings and priests. Maybe you could even climb to the top of a pyramid and look out across the land.

More than a thousand years after the Mayans began building their cities, explorers called *conquistadores* (cohn-kee-stah-DOR-ehz) sailed to Central America from Spain. They took the land from the native people by force. They built new cities and started large farms, forcing the native people to work like slaves. The Mayans' way of life changed overnight.

Today, the Mayan people of Guatemala still struggle to be treated fairly.

The ruins of some Mayan pyramids are hidden deep inside the rain forest.

This class studies hard together. Their teachers are proud of them.

Practice Makes Perfect

Like you, if kids in Central America want to do something well, they have to do it over and over until they get it right. Kids in the highlands have plenty to learn. They practice reading, writing, and math in school. They practice swimming and diving at the beach or pond. They practice sports and games so they can play them well. They practice the type of work they need to do for their families.

Music is an important part of life in Central America. People sing in church and school. Musicians play at celebrations. Everyone likes to listen or dance when good music is playing. If a Central American kid wants to be a good musician, how does he or she do it? Probably

← **This Nicaraguan girl knows how to work on a computer. She uses it to do her schoolwork and help with the family business.**

the same way you do—practice! Playing music isn't easy.

Many jobs that kids do are difficult and important. Most of the time, kids learn new skills by working with parents and other relatives. Some might need to learn how to handle money in a family store. Others must learn to weave fabrics, grow crops, or care for farm animals. Without practice, kids might make mistakes that cost the entire family money. Just like you, these kids know it feels great to do something the right way.

This band in Guatemala practiced a long time before they were ready to perform in public.

All in the Family

Families are as important in Central America as they are in your hometown. Parents and kids do things together and take care of each other. Kids have plenty of help when they are growing up. Everybody in the family helps the younger kids grow and learn. Aunts, uncles, cousins, and grandparents who live nearby help, too. Often everyone lives together in the same house! Even though it's crowded, there is also lots of love.

Central American families do many different things together. They work to grow food that they sell or eat. They care for family members who are very young or very old. They visit relatives and go to church. They weave and sew to make fabrics and clothing. They sell things in the family store or at the town market. They help one another with homework. In volcano country, families talk, laugh, and play together, just like families everywhere.

← **These girls sell nuts, candy, and other snacks to earn money for their families.**

Wearing traditional, brightly colored clothes, a Mayan Indian mother relaxes with her baby.

Helping in Town and All Around

Kids here are always busy helping. Parents need help taking care of younger kids. That means big brothers and sisters have to be responsible. Maybe a big sister takes her little sister to work in the garden. A big brother might take his little brother to the town plaza to play. If there is a baby in the house, older kids help with washing, feeding, and changing diapers. Just like at your house, there are many chores. From fetching the water at the village water tank to sweeping up ash when a volcano erupts, Central American kids have lots to do around the house.

← **A boy and his father gather wood to use at home.**

Kids do chores outside the home as well. When it's time to collect money for charity, kids do it. When people are needed to help carry things in the religious procession, kids get the job. When the church bell ringer wants assistants to ring the church bell, he will probably ask a kid.

Someday, these kids will grow up to have families of their own. By working hard and helping out when they are young, they are learning how to be smart parents and good members of their community. You might have to do different jobs at your house, but you do them for the same reason that kids in Central America do — because your family needs your help!

Time for a wash! When little sister needs bathing, big sister helps out. →

25

Going to Church

Most families in Central America are members of the Catholic Church. Others belong to Protestant and other kinds of churches. Some Mayans worship in special ways they learned from their ancestors. No matter what kind of religion people practice, church and worship are important to most people who live in volcano country.

Mestizos (meh-STEE-sos) are people who have both Mayan and Spanish ancestors. Most

A girl helps out during a religious celebration.

Inside the church, people gather for a special service.

Central Americans are mestizos. In their Catholic churches, mestizos combine traditional Catholic beliefs with Mayan customs. Often, Mayans, mestizos, Spanish, and others all live together in a single town. Religion helps unite these different people in the community.

For people in volcano country, many of the most important things in life happen in church. Holy days are often celebrated inside a church. Holidays such as Christmas and Easter begin and end with celebrations in church. People get married in church. When someone dies, the funeral service is held in church. Many people go to priests and pastors at church to get help, guidance, and advice.

When people wonder about their lives, they often find the answers from someone at church. There are lots of big questions to think about. Where did we come from? How does the universe work? Why are we here? Just as you do, kids in volcano country wonder about lots of things.

Like this celebration in Guatemala, most religious parades begin inside a church. →

EL SERMÓN DE MARÍA
HACED LO QUE JESÚS OS DIG

Celebrations!

In the villages and towns near volcanoes, people celebrate many special days with *fiestas* (fee-EST-ahs) or parties. On fiesta days, families often gather together at the church. The band plays music, and sweet-smelling incense fills the air. At many fiestas, a parade marches through the streets while fireworks crackle and pop all day long and into the night.

At certain fiestas, kids dress up in costumes, just as you might during Halloween. There are pirates, princesses,

During the celebration of San Guadalupe, kids dress in costumes.

In some Spanish-speaking countries, Santa Claus is called "San Nicolas."

cowboys—maybe even a super-hero or two! Kids play with balloons and enjoy fruity drinks. Fiestas are exciting celebrations, full of color, smells, noise, and activity.

Birthdays are other great occasions for celebration. The whole family gathers for a party. At many birthday parties, each child will take turns wearing a blindfold while trying to break the *piñata* (peen-YAH-tah). Parents hide candies inside the piñatas.

The biggest celebration of the year comes at Holy Week, the week before Easter. Many people take vacations or visit relatives during this time. Lots of towns have special celebrations throughout the week, ending with a big fiesta and parade on Easter Sunday.

Celebrations are fun, but they also help people remember serious things. People think of the hard work they do and are glad that it's finished for awhile. They remember friends and family members who have died. They go to church to show their faith and respect. Fiesta time is valuable for everyone in Central America.

Masks are a fun part of some celebrations in volcano country.

Good-Bye and Adios to Volcano Country

Now you know something about the kids who live near the volcanoes of Central America. Just like children all around the world, they are similar to you in lots of ways. They work hard at the jobs their families need them to do. They enjoy playing games and sports with friends. They explore nature and learn new things.

For many of these kids, life is not easy. Most families are poor. Often, kids who want to finish school and find good jobs, never get the chance. But most kids have families that are full of love. They celebrate joyous fiestas together throughout the year. If you visit Central America someday, you'll meet friendly kids who are glad to meet you.

"*Adios!*" say the children. "Farewell!"

And what about all those huge, rumbling volcanoes? No one pays much attention to them. After all, the boys and girls of the Central American highlands are kids who walk on volcanoes, not run away from them!

As a girl watches steam rise into the air, a volcano watches over the land.

31

Glossarized Index